MINUTE
meditations

quick practices for 5, 10 or 20 minutes

Madonna Gauding

An Hachette UK Company
www.hachette.co.uk

First published in Great Britain in 2021 by Pyramid,
an imprint of Octopus Publishing Group Ltd.
Carmelite House
50 Victoria Embankment
London, EC4Y 0DZ
www.octopusbooks.co.uk

ISBN: 978-0-7537-3460-5

A CIP catalogue record for this book is available from the British
Library

Printed and bound in China

10 9 8 7 6 5 4 3 2

Publisher: Lucy Pessell
Designer: Hannah Coughlin
Junior Editor: Sarah Kennedy
Editorial Assistant: Emily Martin
Senior Production Controller: Emily Noto

CONTENTS

INTRODUCTION

If you are new to meditation, you will feel comfortable with this book. And if you are an experienced meditator, you may find renewed inspiration here.

Whether you are a beginner or have been meditating for some time, this book offers a broad collection of simple, effective meditations for enriching your daily life and deepening your spiritual practice. All are clearly explained, with easy-to-follow instructions to help you.

WHY MEDITATE?

If you have never meditated before, the idea may seem a little intimidating. You may think you need a special room with an elaborate altar, incense, candles, a special meditation cushion and a large block of uninterrupted, quiet time.

In this book, you may be surprised and pleased to learn, there are ways to meditate throughout your day that require very little time (and although nice to have, no altar or meditation room), and can be done anywhere. In 5, 10 or 20 minutes, you can nourish and renew yourself – at home, at work, at school or while walking in the park – wherever you are, whenever you can take a very short break in your day. *Minute Meditations* offers an immediate, powerful antidote to stress and the common feeling among us of being overwhelmed. It provides ways to recharge your mind and body with very little intrusion into your daily schedule. Because it relieves stress, meditation is a wonderful health practice. Because it offers ways to become more conscious of your thought patterns, your spiritual attunement to yourself and the universe will grow. If practised on a daily basis, even for a very short period of time, these short meditations can have a big impact on your quality of life.

If you are a long-time meditator, you will find these powerful short meditations will augment your longer meditations sessions. You can drop into a meditative state whenever you want, wherever you are, without having to carve out a half hour or hour of your time. If you have trouble finding time for your longer meditation sessions, *Minute Meditations* will keep your mind attuned, acclimated to meditative practice, and ready for when you do have the time.

HOW TO START

Start with the 5 minute meditations and choose a meditation that appeals to you. Try practising it when you first wake in the morning, or before you fall asleep. Or you can take 5 minutes in your car, in the parking lot, before you start your day at work. During your lunch break, give yourself 5 minutes to relieve the stress of the morning and prepare yourself for your work in the afternoon.

When you have experimented with a few 5 minute meditations in different settings, try a few 10 minute meditations that appeal to you. After a while, with some experimentation, you will discover creative ways to practise at work, at home, or in other settings. You will become comfortable with practising wherever you are during your day. Keep this small book with you or memorize some of the meditations that speak to you.

When you have experimented for a while with 5 and 10 minute meditations, try a 20 minute meditation. You can try these at home in your own meditation space, while sitting in a park, during your commute on the bus or train, or when on vacation. You will find integrating meditation into your life is much easier than you think.

MEDITATION TOPICS

Each one of the 5, 10 or 20 minute meditations will be focused on one of the following six topics.

Calming and Centring: These meditations will help you address stress, anxiety and rumination over work, money, and relationships to help you bring more serenity into your life. Calming and centring meditations include various breathing practices and the experience of nature to bring your body and mind into a peaceful, relaxed state.

Healing Body, Mind and Spirit: These meditations incorporate visualization, yoga, and other techniques to encourage physical, mental and emotional healing. You will discover meditation to be an extremely powerful ally in healing every aspect of your life.

Love and Compassion: In this category, you will explore ways to generate love and compassion for yourself and others, and you will meditate on the meaning of unconditional love to help you bring that quality into your relationships.

Living Mindfully: Our minds are continually busy with thought. That habit of constantly thinking, jumping from one thought to another, keeps us from experiencing the present in all its joy and beauty. These meditations will help you be more mindful of what you are thinking and doing at any given moment.

Problem Solving: We all have problems. Meditation can help you solve problems by helping you tap into sources of wisdom. Through meditation you may discover a path forward that you may not have considered.

Manifesting Your Dreams and Connecting to the Divine: Meditation will help you manifest your dreams, not just for yourself but for the highest good of all. Meditation will help you connect to whatever or whomever you feel represents divinity. This can be an entity or reality outside of yourself or your own higher power.

MEDITATIONS FOR...

5 MINUTE
meditations

It may not sound like much, but 5 minutes a day can do wonders to aid mindfulness and wellbeing. Taking just a few short moments to connect with your thoughts can improve your state of mind, helping you to get back on track. It's also a great way to familiarize yourself with the practise of meditation if you're new to it.

NINE-ROUND BREATHING

This is a breathing and purification practice, useful for balancing your mind and reducing negative thoughts. Practise Nine-Round Breathing before any meditation session or when you want to reduce negative emotions triggered by situations at home or at work.

1. Visualize your body as completely empty and transparent. During the first round of breathing, inhale through your left nostril keeping the right closed with your left index finger.

2. Imagine breathing in and filling your body with pure white light. While exhaling, imagine that any obsessions with sex or material possessions leave via your right nostril in the form of black smoke. Repeat three times.

3. Hold your left nostril closed with your right index finger and inhale pure white light through your right nostril. You are now clearing your anger and hatred, which leave via your left nostril in the form of black smoke. Repeat three times.

4. Breathe in white light through both nostrils. Breathe out any ignorance or mental confusion in the form of black smoke. Imagine this smoke leaving your body at the point between your eyebrows, which meditation masters refer to as your third eye or wisdom eye. Repeat three times.

EMERGENCY BREATH MEDITATION

Breath meditation – a simple and profound meditation –
can be practised any time you feel overwhelmed by stress.
You can meditate at home, at work, at the doctor's office,
before taking an exam, or in your car before the big
interview. Taking 5 minutes to meditate on your breath
will make situations that seem frightening, hopeless
or out of control, suddenly workable.

1. Wherever you are, sit with your back as straight as possible, your shoulders level and relaxed, your feet flat on the ground and your chin parallel to the floor. Lower your eyes and focus about a metre (three feet) in front of you or, if you prefer, close your eyes.

2. Breathe normally through your nose, using your abdomen rather than your chest.

3. Each time you inhale, feel your breath travelling through your entire body. With each breath let yourself feel more relaxed, embodied and grounded.

4. After 5 minutes or so, end your session.

FLOWING WATER

The sound of flowing water connects you with the
flow of nature and reminds you that change is a natural
part of life. The soothing sound blocks out harsh noises
and your own mental chatter. Try this meditation
whenever you have been cooped up for a long period
of time in your home or office building where the air
is not particularly fresh or healthy.

1. Sit on a cushion, a chair or the ground near a source
    of flowing water – a fountain, a river, a stream,
    a waterfall.

2. Breathe normally and focus on the sound of the
    water for 5 minutes. Try to empty your mind of all
    thoughts. When thoughts intervene return your
    focus to the sound of the flowing water.

3. With each in-breath, allow the sound of the water
    to deepen your relaxation in body and mind. Notice
    if you feel better physically when you are next to
    flowing water.

4. When you feel ready end your meditation.

MICROCOSMIC ORBIT

This little-known Taoist meditation is a great way to heal
your organs and maintain good health. Read through the
steps first, then practise the meditation.

1. Sit on a straight-baked chair with your feet flat on the floor. Calm your mind and regulate your breath. When your mind is settled, turn your attention to your navel. Visualize a pocket of energy glowing in your umbilical region. If possible, try to feel the energy. Use your mind to guide it down to the perineum and back up through the coccyx.

2. When you feel the energy has gone through this area, visualize it rising up to where your ribs meet your spine. Now visualize it rising right up to the base of your skull.

3. When the energy goes through this spot, press your tongue against your palate. Next visualize the energy reaching your crown. Then focus attention on the spot between your eyebrows and draw energy down from your crown and out through the point between your brows.

4. Let the energy sink down through the spot between your eyebrows, through your palate and tongue into your throat, down to your heart. Draw it down through your solar plexus, into your naval area once again. Repeat the cycle as many times as you wish.

5. End your meditation by affirming that your organs have been healed and rejuvenated.

SUN SALUTATION

This famous yoga asana, Surya-Namaskar, will get you moving early in the day. Practise this as a healing meditation first thing in the morning to engender a sense of gratitude and purpose.

1. Stand with your feet hip-width apart, hands by your sides.

2. Inhale, raise your arms overhead, and arch your back as far as feels comfortable.

3. As you exhale, bend forward and rest your hands beside your feet. Inhale and step the right leg back with hands still on the floor.

4. Exhale and step the left leg back. Now you are in a push-up position with arms fully extended. Hold the position and inhale. Exhale and lower yourself as if coming down from a push up. Only your hands and feet should touch the floor.

5. Inhale and stretch forward and up, bending at the waist. Use your arms to lift your torso, but only bend back as far as is comfortable.

6. Exhale, lift and push your hips back and up with your head facing down between your straight legs

7. Inhale and step your right foot forward. Exhale, bring your left foot forward, and pull your head to your knees. Inhale and stand tall while keeping your arms extended over your head. Exhale and lower your arms to your sides. Repeat the sequence, stepping back with the left leg first.

TAP AWAY

There are many new therapeutic techniques for dealing with stress based on tapping opposite sides of your body. This one is simple and forms the basis of a powerful meditation. Practise this technique whenever you are suffering with anxiety caused by something in your past or something you are currently worried about.

1. Sit in a straight-backed chair with your back straight and your hands resting on your thighs.

2. Think about the cause of your anxiety. Visualize as clearly as possible the event, people or situation and fully feel your distress.

3. Now using your index finger, begin to tap lightly, first on one thigh then the other, alternating back and forth. Do this rhythmically, at a speed that feels comfortable to you, and that you can sustain for 5 minutes. As you tap, keep visualizing the source of your stress.

4. After 5 minutes you should feel a lessening of your anxiety. If the anxiety is still partially there, repeat the exercise another time. If it is not completely gone after the second exercise, try again, only this time move your eyes from side to side.

TONGLEN FOR YOURSELF

Tonglen is a practice for developing compassion.
In the Tonglen visualization, you receive – with an
open heart – the suffering of others and give selflessly
all of your love, joy and wellbeing to them. But it is always
wise to practise Tonglen for yourself too. Practise
Tonglen for yourself when you are having difficulties
or problems with chronic self-hatred. You can practise
this meditation at any time, anywhere.

1. For formal practice, sit with a straight back on your cushion or chair in a quiet place. Or you can practise whenever and wherever you like.

2. Focus on any difficulties you are currently experiencing. If you are sad and regretful or if you are stressed about money, bring that problem to your full awareness.

3. Breathe your problems and difficulties into your heart.

4. Visualize your difficulties being dissolved and transformed. Now see them ride out on your out-breath as happiness and joy, luminosity and fearlessness.

5. Practise Tonglen with the hope of healing your attitude and restoring yourself to wholeness. Continue exhaling and inhaling, riding your breath in this way for 5 minutes.

TONGLEN FOR OTHERS

After practising the Tonglen meditation for yourself
(see page 28), this Tonglen meditation will teach you how
to practise it in order to develop feelings of compassion
for others. Practise Tonglen for those close to you when
you become aware they are suffering.

1. Sit with a straight back on your chair or practise spontaneously anytime and anywhere you want. Breathe for a few minutes to calm your mind. Then imagine having unlimited love and compassion.

2. Think of someone close to you, who you know is suffering from life problems or illness. Visualize the person in front of you.

3. Breathe in their suffering in the form of black smoke and let it gather in your heart. Be willing to take it on and remove it from them. As it reaches your heart imagine it dissolving all your self-centredness.

4. Now breathe out love, joy and compassion. Don't hold anything back. When you first start this practice, you may have some difficulty visualizing taking in other peoples' suffering and giving away all your joy and happiness to them. But over time, this will change. You will discover that you have an abundance of positive resources, more than you can imagine

5. Continue taking and sending on your breath for 5 minutes or longer if you like. End when you are ready.

UNCONDITIONAL LOVE

Most often our love is conditional – based on whether
our loved ones behave the way we would like or support
us in our endeavours. But a better love is one without
conditions – we love them as they are, regardless of what
they do. This applies especially to our close friends and
family members. Practise this meditation anytime you
feel there are issues in your relationships.

1. Sit on a cushion or chair in your private meditation space. Begin by watching your breath and calming body and mind.

2. Bring to mind your partner or other loved one. List any conditions you have that limit your love for them. For example, you may find you love them on the condition that they make a lot of money, buy you flowers for special events or wear certain clothes. Note how these conditions, while seeming rational, constrict your heart. Note how this doesn't sound like love, more like a demand that your needs be met.

3. Now visualize giving your loved one complete freedom to be and do what they want. Does this frighten you, make you sad or change how you feel about them? Bring to mind the qualities you love about this person. Perhaps you love their energy, their courage, their kindness and their ability to respond to others.

4. Imagine them not being with you or available to meet your needs and loving them anyway. Feel your heart expand as you accept and love them wholeheartedly, regardless of what they do or don't do.

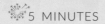

MONKEY MIND

While you are awake, you are thinking constantly.
Your mind may jump from one thought to another,
like a monkey leaping from branch to branch.
This meditation helps you to be more mindful of
what you are thinking, and helps when you are
chronically distracted, feeling scattered in your
thinking or having difficulty concentrating.

1. Take a few deep breaths to signal to yourself that you are going to focus on this meditation. Immediately begin to watch your thoughts. Notice how quickly and seamlessly your mind jumps from one idea, impression and thought to another.

2. Think back to a few minutes ago and try to remember what you were thinking. Trace how you got to what you are thinking now.

3. Look at a watch or a clock for 60 seconds. Make hash marks with a pencil every time your thoughts change during the minute.

4. Bring this new awareness into your daily life. Try to be more mindful of what you are thinking, rather than getting lost in thought.

YOU HAVE A BODY

Meditating on mindfulness of physical sensations allows
you to become more aware of your body. If you have been
split off mentally from your body, this meditation will
help you reconnect your mind with your physical self.

1. Sit on a cushion or a chair keeping your back as straight as possible, yet relaxed. Calm your mind by observing your breath.

2. Shift the focus on your breath to another part of your body. Choose a spot that is easy to feel, like your neck or your knee. Focus all your awareness on that spot. Try to merge with any sensations you may feel.

3. Observe the sensation without judging it as pleasant or unpleasant.

4. Is the sensation a tightness, a burning or a tingling? Is it a combination of many sensations? Do they change over time? Keep your awareness on the spot. If thoughts intrude, return your focus to the spot you have chosen.

5. If you want, switch to another part of your body and repeat the same exercise. When ready, end your meditation. Try to bring this mindfulness of your body into your daily life.

SPACE CADET

Do you have a tendency to "space-out" when you feel
overwhelmed by problems and responsibilities?
Try this meditation if you have difficulty staying aware
of what is going on around you, or if you have run into
problems because you were not paying attention.

1. Stand barefoot on a wooden floor with your feet shoulder-width apart. Keep your spine straight and shoulders level and relaxed. Your arms can hang loosely at your sides, slightly away from your body, as if you are holding an egg under each armpit. Feel your feet on the smooth floor.

2. Keep your eyes open and breathe naturally. Without turning your head try to take in as much as you can through your senses. Notice the colour of the furniture, the shape and textures of objects in the room. Observe the light and shadows. Notice any smells and feel the temperature. Now pay attention to any sounds. Do you hear the sound of a fan or the motor humming in your refrigerator?

3. Mediate in this way for 5 minutes. If you feel nervous to be this aware, ask yourself why. Practise being this attentive to your environment on a daily basis. Then try being this attentive to the people you are with.

GET OUT OF DEBT

The habit of living beyond your means may be dragging you down mentally, physically and spiritually. This meditation will help you to find the courage to get yourself out of debt. If you have a problem with credit-card debt, practise this meditation on a weekly basis until you are out of debt.

1. Sit on a cushion or chair in your meditation space. Light a candle to help you focus.

2. Gather your records together and add up how much you are in debt. Say the amount out loud: 'I am [however much] in debt'. Let that fact resonate in your consciousness. How do you feel saying that fact out loud? If you feel numb or if you feel fear, anxiety or shame, note it. How does your body feel when you say the amount out loud? Do you experience a feeling of tension or is your breathing constricted?

3. After admitting to yourself the extent of your debt, generate a sense of compassion for your difficulties in controlling your spending. From this place of compassion commit to getting out of debt, no matter how long it takes. Ask your higher power to help you control your spending and give you the courage to seek professional help if you need it.

4. End your meditation by making a promise to your higher power that you will stop spending on credit and will reduce the amount you owe every month by paying off some of the balance.

FACING THE MIRROR

Everyone has difficulties and problems that persist over time. You are not alone in this. It is time to face your problems directly, with courage and honesty. Try this meditation when you feel you are avoiding your problems.

1. Find a time when you can be alone. Stand in front of your bathroom mirror or a full-length mirror.

2. Look at your reflection. Speaking out loud, tell yourself three things you like about yourself. It could be that you are a good listener, a very intelligent person or a great cook.

3. Love the person looking back at you. Tell yourself you know you are struggling, but it is important to admit to the problem that has been dragging you down.

4. Out loud, in a clear voice, tell yourself the problem you have been avoiding. For example, you might say "I am overweight, and I need to lose it for my health and wellbeing". Repeat your statement three times.

5. Now commit to taking a step to resolve your problem within the next 24 hours. Say out loud what you plan to do. Repeat it three times.

6. Close your meditation by congratulating yourself for your courage and honesty.

ACCOUNTABILITY

It is easy to blame others for your problems. But the habit of assigning blame for your own actions – on others, the weather, the economy or anything else – is dishonest and disempowering. If you are playing the blame game, you are only hurting yourself. When you don't feel accountable for your actions, you deprive yourself of the opportunity to learn and grow. Try this meditation if you find yourself blaming others for your problems.

1. Sit on a cushion or chair in your meditation space.
    Take a few deep breaths.

2. Think of a situation or project where things went
    wrong, not because of something you did, but
    because of someone's actions. For example, you
    may have finished an important proposal with a
    deadline of the next day, given it to an assistant to
    send it overnight, but the assistant failed to do the
    job. When your boss is furious, you in turn blame
    your assistant. How do you feel when you blame your
    assistant?

3. Now take the viewpoint that you were accountable
    for the proposal being written and delivered on time.
    How does this feel? Do you feel more empowered?
    When you feel fully accountable, you can learn from
    your mistakes. Perhaps next time you will get the
    proposal done early and check to see that it was sent
    a day ahead.

4. Think of a similar situation in which you blamed
    someone else for your failure. Reconsider that
    situation and this time take full responsibility. What
    did you learn? How were you empowered by being
    accountable?

MAKE THE LEAP

You may want to manifest your dreams, but fear may be holding you back. Try this meditation to help you take the leap and make your vision a reality, or if you feel ready to manifest a dream but are afraid to move forward.

1. Sit on a cushion or chair in your meditation space. Take a few deep breaths to calm and centre yourself.

2. Bring to mind a dream you would like to manifest. Ask yourself why you have not moved forward to make it a reality. Explore your beliefs about yourself and how they may be getting in your way. For example, if you have always wanted to learn to ride a horse but are afraid of getting hurt or you feel it is too extravagant for your lifestyle, or more fun than you deserve, then examine those beliefs and counter them with new ones. As an example, tell yourself millions of people ride horses without getting hurt, it is money well spent on something that feeds your soul, and of course you deserve to be happy and enjoy your life.

3. End your meditation by committing to take the first step toward making your dream a reality. It may mean a phone call, doing research, signing up for a class or quitting your job. Whatever it is make sure you make the leap into your future and your happiness.

DEVOTION

There are many spiritual traditions that rely on devotion as a path to spiritual fulfilment. Use this meditation to explore devotion as a direct experience of Divine love.

1. Sit on a cushion or chair in your meditation space. Meditate on relinquishing your attachment to superficial concerns that may be getting in the way of your spiritual path. For example, if you are obsessed with clothes and how you look, you may contemplate how this may not be serving you spiritually.

2. Immerse yourself in unselfish, unceasing love for the Divine. On a devotional path everything is an expression of the Divine's love. Your stress, pain and anxiety arise from not seeing the world or yourself as worthy of love. Let go of your ego's painful struggle for recognition and dominance and surrender to Divine love.

3. Imagine every breath you take in is love, and every breath out is compassion. You are an expression of the Divine's love and his or her love flows through you. Consider forming a relationship with a teacher, in whatever form he or she takes. Imagine you are devoted to your teacher and the teachings which empower you to develop on your spiritual path.

4. End your session by meditating on how you might practise devotion on your current spiritual path.

BUDDHA NATURE

Buddhism teaches that you have Buddha nature.
In other words, you have the capacity to become
enlightened and become a Buddha yourself. Try this
meditation if you are feeling negative about yourself
or your potential to develop spiritually.

1. Sit on a cushion or chair in your meditation space. Take a few deep breaths and relax your body and mind.

2. Contemplate your own Buddha nature in the form of a seed. Imagine that you begin to "water" this seed with meditation on patience, love, compassion and other positive topics. Imagine that you strive to be a more positive, loving and compassionate person. Now you have what is called a "growing Buddha nature".

3. Over time see yourself slowly eliminating your negative habits and replacing them with positive ones. Imagine your thoughts and actions becoming more positive every day. Imagine how it would feel to become a Buddha, to be enlightened.

4. Imagine having no negativity, no suffering and perfect wisdom and compassion. Imagine being able to help all beings. Sit quietly and contemplate what that might be like.

5. If you choose, commit to growing your own Buddha nature by increasing your positive virtues and eliminating your negative habits.

10 MINUTE
meditations

This section is perfect if you're feeling in need of a slightly longer break, but still don't have the time to drop everything you're doing. These slightly longer meditations will provide effective results, but don't require intense concentration.

WATCHING YOUR BREATH

This is one of the simplest of all meditations,
yet one of the most powerful and rewarding.
Meditating on the breath each day provides
a foundation for all other forms of meditation.

1. Sit cross-legged on a cushion with your bottom slightly raised. If you can't sit cross-legged, sit on a chair.

2. Keep your back straight, your shoulders level and relaxed and your chin parallel to the floor. Lower your eyes and focus about a metre (three feet) in front of you. Rest your hands gently on your knees.

3. Breathe normally through your nose, using your abdomen rather than your chest. Check your posture and relax any part of your body that is tense.

4. Begin counting your breath on each exhalation; when you reach ten, begin again.

5. After 10 minutes or so, end your session.

THOUGHT CLOUDS

Thoughts inevitably arise when trying to focus your mind, and can sometimes be distracting. Labelling your thoughts as they emerge will help you to refocus on and calm your mind. Try this meditation for 10 minutes at a time, morning and evening.

1. Sit cross-legged on a cushion with your bottom slightly raised. If you can't sit cross-legged, sit on a chair.

2. Keep your back straight, your shoulders level and relaxed and your chin parallel to the floor.

3. Lower your eyes and focus about a metre (three feet) in front of you. Rest your hands gently on your knees.

4. Breathe normally through your nose, using your abdomen rather than your chest. Check your posture and relax any part of your body that is tense.

5. Begin counting your breath and when you reach ten begin again. When thoughts intervene label them as "thinking" and return to concentrate on your breath.

6. Meditate in this way for about 10 minutes.

7. Try this meditation for a week. See if you notice how changeable and ephemeral your thoughts are.

DISTRACTED MIND

When trying to focus our minds, distractions can
originate outside ourselves in the form of sounds,
lights or smells. Labelling them helps you return
to focusing your mind. Try this meditation for
10 minutes, both morning and evening.

1. Sit cross-legged on a cushion with your bottom slightly raised. If you can't sit cross-legged, sit on a chair. Keep your back straight, your shoulders level and relaxed and your chin parallel to the floor. Lower your eyes and focus about a metre (three feet) in front of you. Rest your hands gently on your knees.

2. Breathe normally through your nose, using your abdomen rather than your chest. Check your posture and relax any part of your body that is tense.

3. Begin counting your breath on each exhalation and when you reach ten, begin again.

4. Notice if you are distracted by anything external such as the sound of a car starting, your housemate closing a door, cooking smells from the kitchen or changes in the temperature of your room.

5. Notice how you feel, label the distraction and return to focusing on your breath.

6. Try this variation of breath meditation, both morning and evening, for a week. Keep track of your distractions and reactions.

7. Notice if your reaction to external distraction differs from internal thought distraction.

8. Notice if your irritation lessens over time.

NECTAR WASHING

Visualization is a powerful tool for healing body, mind and spirit. Use this meditation to ward off illness or if you are ill. This is also a wonderful meditation to practise on a regular basis for maintaining your good general health.

1. Sit down for a few minutes and write down any health problems you have, however small or serious. Now sit on a cushion or chair in your usual meditation space. Begin watching your breath for a few minutes.

2. Think of all the health problems you listed. See them as black spots residing in various parts of your body. Note how your health problems hinder your life, feel any emotions that arise.

3. Visualize that you are near a beautiful waterfall in a warm, tropical location. No one is around. Undress and find a place where you can sit directly under the flow. Imagine that the water is not ordinary water, but a heavenly nectar that heals illness and prevents disease.

4. Visualize all your health problems being cleansed by this nectar. Feel the nectar not only flowing over your body but through it as well, taking with it all the black spots you visualized earlier.

5. Affirm to yourself that your body is now free of health problems. Get up from your seat under the waterfall, dry off and put on your clothes. Leave this beautiful site knowing that you are in vibrant health. Know that you can return to it whenever you want.

HOLD THE OPPOSITES

You may find yourself locked into dualistic thinking –
everything has to be right or wrong, black or white,
good or bad. This meditation helps you learn to tolerate
a more realistic view of life. If you find yourself angry
and fearful, wanting simplistic, clear answers or
demanding that things be done "your way", try this
meditation to help you tolerate life as it really is.

1. Sit on a cushion or straight-backed chair in a quiet place where you can be alone. Meditate by watching your breath for about 5 minutes.

2. Think of a situation where you have been miserable because you wanted something to be a certain way and the other person wanted another outcome. Pay attention to your emotions. The first one to arise may be anger. Check to see if underneath the anger you feel fear. What will you lose if you let both points of view exist simultaneously?

3. Imagine that you are alone on a desert island with that person and your survival depends on both of you having your needs met. Imagine a creative way to compromise so that each of you has at least part of what you desire.

4. After you have reached your compromise solution whereby both you and the other person can be "right" and have something of what you want, notice if you feel less stress and more contentment.

FEED YOUR DEMONS

If you suffer from addictions – drugs, alcohol,
food, sex, Internet or whatever – you are probably
running away from pain and not nurturing yourself
in appropriate ways. Try this meditation to learn
how to take better care of yourself and to begin
healing from your troublesome addictions.

1. Sit on a cushion or straight-backed chair in a quiet, private place.

2. Bring to mind what you consider to be your most troublesome addiction. Now see your addiction as a person other than yourself. For instance, if your addiction is to cigarettes, you might see your addiction as a thin, sallow-skinned man who is tense and hunched over.

3. Ask the person you have created what they are feeling and what they need that they are not getting. Your smoking character might tell you he wants to relax, clear his lungs and quit racing around all the time.

4. After you have had a conversation with your "demon" imagine you are responsible for their care and visualize helping them heal. Think of at least one way you could help them feel better and stop abusing themselves. Now apply this nurturing solution to your own life.

LOVE YOURSELF

Self-hatred is common in our culture. This meditation
will help you counteract any feelings of self-hatred,
including shame or low self-esteem. Try this
meditation when you become aware of self-hatred.

1. Sit on a cushion or chair in a quiet place. Visualize your higher power sitting in front of you. It could be Jesus, Buddha, Shakti, Mohammed or just a wise form of yourself.

2. Imagine your higher power smiling at you with great love and compassion, accepting you as you are. Understand that he or she does not demand that you "fix" anything about yourself to deserve his or her love. Know that he or she wants you to accept yourself exactly as you are and treat yourself with kindness and respect as they already do.

3. Take a moment to feel their unconditional love and acceptance.

4. Thank your higher power for reminding you to be kind toward yourself. Tell him or her that with their help and encouragement, you will refrain from self-hatred and encourage yourself to accept yourself exactly as you are. Promise that you will try to live your life with complete self-acceptance and self-love.

FORGIVENESS

There is nothing more difficult or more rewarding than
forgiveness. You can forgive yourself and others once
you have done the emotional work necessary to process
your feelings and let go of always having to be "right".
This meditation on forgiveness is grounded in the reality
that you and others are in a constant state of change.
Although it may appear so, you are not the person you
were yesterday or even a minute ago, nor is the person
who harmed you. Forgiveness helps you shed your pain
and anger, and opens your heart once again.

1. Sit on a cushion or chair in your meditation space. If you have an altar, meditate on your chosen higher power. Light a candle and make simple offerings of flowers or fruit. Ask for help in forgiving the person who harmed you.

2. Recall the event in which you felt harmed. If your first emotion is anger, look underneath for hurt. As you think about and feel what happened, try not to vilify the other person. Simply admit how you are feeling.

3. Now think of the other person. See them as a whole person who is more than their actions and who is changing every moment. Understand that they did what they did because they thought it would make them happy and help them avoid suffering. Their motivations are no different from yours.

4. Forgive the person who hurt you. Say this out loud. Wish them to be happy and free of suffering. Open yourself to the possibility of healing your relationship in the present. If that's not possible, simply let go of your anger and pain. See it as a large, heavy suitcase that you refuse to carry any longer.

5. Thank your higher power for helping you see the bigger picture.

FOUR IMMEASURABLES

This meditation will help you feel more kindness and
compassion toward yourself and toward others. It is
a wonderful antidote to the nightly news; wishing that
an immeasurable number of beings have immeasurable
love, compassion and joy. You will need to memorize
the following prayer for this meditation:

May all beings have happiness
May all beings be free from suffering
May all beings find joy that has never known suffering
May all beings be free from attachment and hatred.

1. Sit on a cushion or chair in your meditation space. Meditate on your breath for a few minutes to calm and centre yourself.

2. Recite out loud the first line of the prayer: "May all beings have happiness." Feel your intention that all beings have your unconditional love. Include yourself in this wish. Accept them and yourself exactly as they and you are.

3. Move to the second line and say it out loud, "May all beings be free from suffering." Imagine that you have infinite compassion and wish all beings, including yourself, to be free from suffering of any kind. Bring to mind any form of suffering. It could be someone with cancer, or your own suffering from illness or addiction. Feel a great urgency to help them and yourself.

4. Recite the third line: "May all beings find joy that has never known suffering." Imagine that all beings have enlightenment, the ultimate spiritual development in Buddhism. Feel the depression of all beings, including yourself, lifting and being eradicated. Imagine they and you are in a blissful, happy, unselfish, enlightened state.

5. Recite the fourth line: "May all beings be free from attachment and hatred." Imagine all beings, regardless of who they are, as worthy of love and compassion. Know this equanimity is the basis for the first three wishes – unconditional, altruistic love, compassion and pure joy.

GLASS HALF-FULL

It's easy to take what you have for granted and be
chronically dissatisfied. Focusing on what blessings
you have can transform your mind and your life.

1. Find time to be alone in a place where you will not be disturbed. Sit in any way that makes you comfortable and have a notebook and pen nearby. Write down everything you want that you don't have. Then write down ten things you are grateful for.

2. Generate a sincere feeling of gratitude for each item on your list you are grateful for. If it's your health, feel thankful for your good fortune. If you have a car, no matter what condition, be sincerely grateful to have transportation. If you have a partner, think of their wonderful qualities and be grateful they are part of your life.

3. After you have gone through your list, sit quietly and thank yourself, the Divine, the universe, or whomever or whatever you choose, for the gifts you have been given. Resolve, on a daily basis, to be mindful and grateful for the blessings you have.

WHAT ARE YOU THINKING?

Noting the content of your thoughts when you meditate
on your breath will help you to discover patterns in your
thinking and be more mindful of your thought processes.
Try this for 10 minutes, morning and evening.

1. Sit cross-legged on a cushion with your bottom
    slightly raised. If you can't sit cross-legged, sit on a
    chair. Keep your back straight, your shoulders level
    and relaxed, your chin parallel to the floor and your
    feet flat on the ground. Lower your eyes and focus
    about a metre (three feet) in front of you. Rest your
    hands gently on your knees.

2. Breathe normally through your nose, using your
    abdomen rather than your chest. Check your posture
    and relax any part of your body that is tense.

3. Begin counting your breath and when you reach ten,
    begin again. When thoughts intervene, note the
    content. For instance, if you thought about money
    problems, silently note "worrying about money"
    and return to counting your breath.

4. Meditate for about 10 minutes. At the end of your
    session write down which thoughts emerged. Do
    this for one week and notice any recurring patterns
    Notice if your thoughts about something or someone
    change over the week.

AUTUMN LEAF

To perceive without bias or judgement is a difficult task for anyone. Unfortunately, labelling and judgements prevent you from experiencing life directly. This simple awareness meditation will help you to experience nature more deeply and joyfully. Practise this meditation when you feel separated from nature and distanced from your own direct experience of life.

1. Walk for a few minutes in the park or woods or along a tree-lined street while focusing on your breath. Try to empty your mind of all thoughts.

2. Stop walking, pick up a fallen leaf and hold it in your hand. Notice if you are judging the leaf in any way – for its appearance, size or colour, or if you are comparing it to another you didn't pick up. Try to let go of any thoughts or judgements about the leaf.

3. Begin by simply taking in the leaf visually as if you were a Martian and had never seen one before. Notice its exquisite shape, colour and the tiny delicate veins spreading from its centre. If it has blemishes from insects or decay, see them as equally beautiful and perfect.

4. Spend time being with the leaf in this way. Try to bring this way of experiencing the leaf to the rest of your life. Notice, when your judging mind drops away, if you feel more relaxed, more fulfilled and more aware of the beauty all around you.

YOU CAN LET GO NOW

Do you have control issues? Has anyone told you
that you are controlling? This meditation will help
you learn to let go , leaving you free to focus on
the parts of your life that truly matter.

1. In preparation, write about three occasions on which you can remember feeling anxiety and wanting to control someone else's behaviour, even if it seemed justified to you at the time. Sit on a cushion or chair in your meditation space. Watch your breath for a few minutes to centre and calm your mind.

2. Choose one of the events you listed. Try to recall it in detail. Feel what you were feeling at the time. Perhaps your partner moved a chair and didn't move it back to where you had placed it when he or she left the room. Was your first feeling one of anger?

3. Ask yourself why it is so important to have things the way you want them, especially since you are sharing your life with another person. If you weren't feeling anger, would you feel fear? Are you afraid something may happen unexpectedly, and you will feel powerless, alone, abandoned? What is the fear behind your need to control?

4. Commit to letting go a little at a time on a daily basis by looking for the fear behind the need for you to control. Relax your grip on things and notice that usually nothing terrible happens. Be kind and patient with yourself in this process.

ASKING FOR HELP

There are more resources for getting help with
psychological, spiritual, health and financial problems
than ever before. But for a variety of reasons – such
as pride, denial and fear – you may find it difficult
to ask for help. This meditation helps you overcome
shame to get the help you need.

1. Sit on a cushion or chair in your meditation space. Breathe deeply for a few minutes. Visualize your higher power in front of you. If you don't believe in a higher power, imagine the wisdom aspect of yourself seated before you.

2. Talk to your higher power about the difficulties you are having. If you are struggling with addiction, tell him or her about it. If you need help to deal with your anger, talk about that. Whatever it is, feel free to tell him or her everything. Visualize your higher power listening to you compassionately and without judgement.

3. Tell your higher power why you have difficulty asking for help. Admit that you need help to overcome your problems and ask for help in making that phone call or getting that appointment. Imagine him or her being very happy that you have finally let go, admitted your problem and have the wisdom to know that you can't deal with it on your own. Imagine your higher power promising to be with you all the way.

4. End your meditation by committing to yourself and your higher power to getting help. Realize this is a sign of your courage and intelligence.

WALKING SOLUTION

Difficult problems sometimes benefit from you
taking a walk to help sort out things in your mind.
Physical movement is energizing. Walking helps move
stagnant energy, promotes better circulation, loosens
stiff joints and encourages creative thinking. If you have
a problem to sort out or a decision to make, try taking
a walk to focus your mind and expand your options.

1. Try to walk in a park or an area with trees. Begin your walk with a few deep breaths to help you relax and focus.

2. Bring to mind the problem that you can't seem to solve. Visualize that each step you take is bringing you closer to a solution. Then focus on your dilemma. For example, if you are not sure if you should go back to college, imagine for a 5 minute stretch that you have made the decision to go back to school. See how that feels to your body and mind.

3. For the next 5 minutes of your walk switch to making the decision not to return to college. Notice how that feels to your body and mind.

4. On your walk back home, invite an unknown solution to arise. For example, another solution besides going or not going to college may be getting on-the-job training, or an apprenticeship. Open yourself to a creative surprise.

FOR THE HIGHEST GOOD

If you have a dream – to start a business, build a house,
write a book – manifest your dream, not just for yourself,
but for the highest good of all. Try this meditation if you
want to start a project or manifest a dream.

1. Sit on a cushion or chair in your meditation space and light a candle. Invite your higher power to join you in this meditation and guide you in your effort to manifest whatever you wish, however small or significant.

2. Think of what it is you would like to manifest. Ask your higher power that this thing, or relationship, or project be for the benefit of all beings, including yourself. Ask that this selfless motivation may guide all your decisions and activities regarding the project.

3. Visualize that your dream has manifested. What would it look like? How would it feel? If it is a business, see yourself in your office having a meeting with your employees. If you want to go into politics, envision yourself giving a campaign speech. Now that it is a reality, is your dream in line with your highest ideals and for the benefit of all?

4. If your dream is indeed for the highest good of all, and you want it to become a reality, write it down and place it in a silver box. Ask your higher power to help you make it a reality.

SOUL WORK

What is it that you are meant to do in this lifetime?
What is your special contribution? Try a little soul work
to explore these very important questions. Practise
this meditation if you feel you are at a crossroads
in your life and need to do something new.

1. In preparation, consider then write down what you care about most deeply and what excites you most intensely.

2. Sit on a cushion or chair in your meditation space. Light a candle and incense to affirm the importance of this moment and the sacredness of your life. Meditate by watching your breath for a few minutes in order to calm your mind and relax your body.

3. Read out loud what you wrote in preparation for this meditation. You may have written that you care most about your family, world peace or the environment. Perhaps science lights a fire in your soul. Let yourself feel any emotions that arise. Are you excited, sad, angry? Did you let your family talk you out of taking a certain job because it didn't have the prestige they felt you should aspire to? Do you spend enough time with your loved ones?

4. Contemplate how you are living your life today and whether it honours what you have written in your statement. There is no fault here, just awareness. Knowing what you care about and what excites you will start you on the path to a more fulfilled life.

SPIRIT OF PLACE

Try this meditation if you want to feel more connected to where you live. This meditation is great if you've been living in the same place for a little while and want to determine whether or not it's time to move on.

1. Stretch out on a mat on the floor and make yourself comfortable. Cover yourself with a blanket if you need to. Breathe deeply for a few minutes and relax all your muscles from your toes to your crown.

2. Visualize your ideal place to live. Describe the town or city or countryside. Is it a large urban area or a small town? Is it in the country in which you now live or somewhere else in the world? What do the buildings look like?

3. Now describe the weather. Is your ideal place in a warmer climate, a temperate one or in a colder region? Imagine yourself dressed appropriately in this place. Describe the people who live in your ideal place. Are they older, younger, progressive, conservative or intellectuals?

4. What sort of house are you living in? Is it large, small, picturesque, cosy, impressive or modest? Who are you living with? Why does this place nurture your body and soul?

5. If you already live in your ideal place, feel grateful for that fact. If you would like to move somewhere else, repeat this meditation until you find your place of spirit.

20 MINUTE
meditations

This section includes longer meditations that may require a little more concentration. They may ask you to connect more fully to your thoughts by getting you to write things down, or by exploring your feelings more deeply.

SPACIOUS MIND

With one thought constantly following another,
your mind may start to feel claustrophobic.
This meditation will help you clear your mental
"space" and give you a much-needed mental holiday.

1. Any time you are feeling stressed and hemmed in by worries or constant thinking, use this meditation.

2. Sit crossed-legged on a cushion or a straight-backed chair with your feet flat on the floor.

3. Begin by focusing on your breath, counting on the out-breath up to ten.

4. After about 5 minutes, stop counting your breath and simply focus on the out-breath for another 2 minutes or so.

5. Become aware of the calmness and space that arises at the end of the out breath.

6. Let yourself float deeper and deeper into that feeling and space. Imagine your breath flowing out into a vast area filled with light. With each breath, let the space get larger and larger.

7. Allow yourself to rest and be in that space in the present.

8. If a thought appears, gently refocus on the spaciousness you have created.

9. Tell yourself that it is okay to just be. Remain in this calm space as long as you like.

10. When you are ready, take a deep breath and end your session.

DANCING FLAME

A single candle flame is a wonderful object on which to focus your mind. It draws your attention, and its warmth, light and beauty are timeless and reassuring. Try this meditation at night whenever you are feeling overwhelmed and fearful about some aspect of your life.

1. Sit on a cushion or chair about a metre (three feet) away from your candle, which should be at eye level. Other lighting in the room should be low but not absent. Try to eliminate any draughts.

2. Begin your session with a 5 minute, Nine-Round Breathing meditation (see page 16).

3. Next, focus on the candle flame and try to empty your mind of all thoughts. With each in-breath, allow the light and warmth of the candle flame to free your mind of any fears, anxiety or insecurity

4. When extraneous thoughts intervene, refocus on the candle flame in front of you.

5. Meditate in this way for an additional 15 minutes.

CENTRING PRAYER
MEDITATION

Most religious traditions practise some form
of centring prayer. This centring prayer meditation
is based on the Christian tradition. Practise
centring prayer meditation whenever you feel
disconnected from your spiritual life.

1. In preparation for this meditation, find a spiritual text that inspires you.

2. Begin reading the book you have selected. Allow a word to emerge from your reading that resonates with you, for example, God, Buddha, Jesus, love or peace. This sacred word expresses your intent for the Sacred to enter your heart and be present in your life.

3. Sit comfortably with your eyes closed and introduce your word inwardly. When you become aware of thoughts or distractions, bring yourself back to your sacred word. Meditate in this way for 20 minutes. At the end of your meditation, remain silent with your eyes closed for a few more minutes. Notice the effects of your centring prayer meditation on your daily life.

WEEDING

If you are a gardener, you understand weeding. Why not make your weeding into a healing, meditative practice? If you don't have a garden, offer to weed for someone else or volunteer with your local parks service.

1. Sit quietly under a tree. Bring to mind any negative habits you may have, such as a bad temper or procrastination. Think of as many as you like. Visualize the weeds in the patch as your negative habits.

2. Get up from under the tree and approach the area you are planning to weed. See that whole area as you or your mind. See the flowers and plants as your positive traits and the weeds as those negative traits that you would like to eliminate.

3. As you begin to weed, try to stay very focused and mindful. When you pull out a weed by its roots, think that you are pulling out your own negative habit by the roots. Continue in this way until all the weeds are removed.

4. Finish by cultivating, feeding and watering the plants and flowers. Think of them as your healing, positive traits that you would like to nurture.

PURIFYING FIRE

Healing is not just for physical illness. If you have
bad habits that affect your mental, emotional, physical
or spiritual health, this meditation will help you
let go of them and start anew.

1. To prepare for this meditation, over a few days, write down any negative habits you have had in the past or have presently. Try to be as honest and thorough as possible. Then write down any feelings you have about your negative habits including any shame or regret.

2. Build a fire in your fireplace or barbecue. Sit on a meditation cushion or a chair nearby. Read your list. Review everything and feel your shame and regret.

3. Visualize your higher power in any form you like. Express your regret for indulging in negative habits and ask for help in living your life in a more positive and constructive way. Feel your higher power's love and acceptance of you as you are. Imagine how your life would be without your negative habits and behaviours.

4. Now place your list into the fire and watch it burn. As your list burns, visualize your negative habits leaving you. Let go of any shame by mentally giving it to the fire and your higher power to be purified. Be kind to yourself as you commit to living a more positive life.

CRISIS EQUALS OPPORTUNITY

When a crisis occurs, you can choose to see it as a disaster
or you can view it as an opportunity. This meditation will
help you focus more positively on the opportunity.

1. Sit on a cushion or chair in your meditation space. Light a candle and if you have an altar, make offerings of flowers and incense to your higher power. Meditate by watching your breath for 10 minutes. When you feel calmer move on to the next step.

2. Tell your higher power what has happened to you. If you feel like crying don't hold back.

3. Now ask your higher power to help you see anything positive that can come out of this crisis. Sit quietly and pray for an expanded vision to help you through this difficult time. Pray that your heart and mind be opened to see the opportunity in this crisis.

4. Now write about what opportunities might present themselves in the midst of this disaster. Perhaps you will learn something new, find a better job or make an entirely fresh start in life. If you have lost all your possessions, focus on the freedom rather than the loss. Even if it seems difficult and you don't really believe what you are writing, write anyway. This will sow the seed for you to genuinely feel the opportunity.

5. Close your meditation by thanking your higher power for helping you through this time.

REPAYING KINDNESS

This is a wonderful meditation for realizing the
kindness of others. It will help you develop compassion
and reduce any self-centredness that may creep into
your thoughts. Try this meditation when you are
feeling alone and struggling.

1. Prepare for this meditation by making a list of everyone who took care of you as a child. You may do this over several days, as names come to you.

2. Sit on your cushion or straight-backed chair. Light a candle in memory of all those who have helped you in your life.

3. Recall the list you made in preparation for your meditation. Begin with your mother and father; then go on to siblings, aunts and uncles, grandparents and cousins, all of whom cared for you in some way. Then think of your teachers, your babysitters, coaches and friends. Think of your first job and the person who hired you. Now consider the farmers who grew the food you ate and the shops that sold the food. Consider your mailman, the garbage man, the police and the firemen who kept you safe. Return to your parents who worked hard for you to have a home, clothes, food, schooling and medical care. Think of your doctors and dentists. Your list is merely the tip of the iceberg. You may want to continue to add to it over time.

4. Generate a sincere sense of gratitude to every person who has helped you in your life. Realize you have been the recipient of so much kindness that it will take lifetimes to repay everyone. Vow to pay back all of that kindness by generating love and compassion for them and for all beings.

INTERCONNECTEDNESS

You are connected to everything and everyone else. This meditation on this important fact will help you counteract feelings of alienation, loneliness or meaninglessness, and increase your sense of loving connection to all beings. Interconnectedness is not just a spiritual idea. Quantum physics finds you are intimately connected to all reality. In preparation for this meditation, buy an apple.

1. Sit on a cushion or chair in your meditation space. Bring your apple with you. Watch your breath for a few minutes and settle your mind.

2. Place the apple on a small table in front of you. Now visualize the seed from which the apple came. Visualize a farmer planting the seed, carefully fertilizing the ground. Clouds come and go, and rain moistens the earth. For years the farmer tends the tree, which is also home to birds and insects, until one day it bears fruit. He hires farm hands to pick the fruit. They pack your apple in a crate with others. The farmer drives your apple to a wholesale market. The wholesaler buys your apple and sells it to your shop. Another driver delivers it to the shop. A shop assistant arranges it for display. You arrive and pick that apple to use for your meditation.

3. Visualize the apple tree and all the people and equipment involved in bringing this one apple to you. You can extend this meditation by tracing every aspect of the process, including the people who built the vehicle that delivered your apple. At every given moment you are connected to an infinite number of beings. You can't exist without them. You are enmeshed in a cosmic web of creation.

4. End your meditation by eating the apple. Feel your connection to every one who made it possible.

BROTHERS AND SISTERS

All religions encourage you to love your parents,
but many do not say as much about siblings. Try this
meditation to heal your sibling relationship and
encourage love between you. This is a great meditation
to practise before a family holiday or event.

1. Sit on your cushion or chair in your meditation space. Place some photos of your siblings on a table in front of you. Light a candle. Meditate on your breath for a few minutes. Now call on your higher power to sit alongside you. Introduce him or her to your siblings.

2. Consider each brother or sister separately and let any feelings emerge. Ask your higher power to help you heal your relationships if they need healing. If they don't, ask that your relationships deepen and strengthen over your lifetimes. If you have unproductive ways of relating that are rooted in your childhood, ask that you be able to shed them and find a new, more mature model.

3. Now recall the positive qualities in each of your brothers and sisters. Ask that you be able to accept and love them exactly as they are.

4. Close your meditation by committing to honour and respect each of your siblings and strengthen the relationships you have with them.

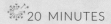
DO I HAVE AN ATTITUDE?

Your attitude toward anyone or anything you encounter is
usually one of either attraction, aversion or indifference.
Using meditation to become aware of your attitudes
leads you to greater mental balance and stability. Try this
meditation when you are feeling particularly judgemental
or self-centred in your dealings with others.

1. Find a quiet place indoors where you can be alone. Sit on a cushion or on a straight-backed chair. Choose a situation or a person on which to focus for this meditation session. Mentally take time to create a vivid and detailed image of the person or situation.

2. As you meditate, allow your feelings to arise and carefully note what they are. Are you feeling anger, sadness, fear, jealousy? Do you feel judgemental? Don't suppress a negative attitude or edit it to what you think you should feel. Accept without judgement any attitude you may have.

3. Ask yourself a series of questions to explore your attitude more closely. Have you always felt this way toward this person? Have you always felt this way in this situation?

4. What led to you feeling this way? What could cause your attitude to change? Note any bodily sensations that arise.

5. As you deepen your understanding of your attitude toward this person or situation, remind yourself that what you feel is only what you feel today. Try to cultivate an attitude of equanimity; that is, not feeling any judgement at all. Remind yourself that attitudes, like everything else, are impermanent and change over time.

DO THE DISHES

How can dish-washing be a meditation? The Zen tradition encourages you to perform every action with total one-pointed awareness and attention. In preparation, have a nice meal. When everyone is finished eating, clear the dishes off the table, and fill your kitchen sink with warm soapy water. Get your scrubber and dishcloth ready. Roll up your sleeves, and begin the meditation opposite.

1. Send everyone out of the kitchen so you can do the dishes alone.

2. Slowly pick up your first dish and begin washing it. Focus exclusively on the dish and the sink. If thoughts intervene, return your focus to what you are doing. When the dish is washed and rinsed, slowly and mindfully place it in the dish drainer. Pick up your next dish and continue in the same manner.

3. Your mind may stray but try to stay in the present and focus on the task at hand. Notice the movement of the water, the soap suds and the comforting warmth of the water as you rinse a plate. Notice the dishes, glasses and pots. Approach the experience as if it is the very first time you have ever washed dishes.

4. Even though it will take much longer than usual, wash every item in this manner. Although exaggerated, try to bring this level of awareness and deliberate attention to everything you do. Keep your mind present and engaged. Notice if you feel more relaxed and peaceful approaching your life in this way.

LIFE IS SHORT

Your life actually goes by in the blink of an eye. Ask any person who is in their eighties or nineties, and they will almost always tell you to make the best of your time. It may sound morbid, but this meditation is actually about helping you live life to the full. If you talk to someone who has recovered from a life-threatening illness, they will often tell you how grateful they are to have had the disease, as it "woke them up" to the preciousness of life.

1. In preparation, read the obituaries in your local paper for today. This may sound unappealing, but it is very helpful to do this once in a while. After you have done so, begin the meditation below.

2. Sit on a cushion or a chair in a quiet place where you can be alone.

3. Note your age and how many years you think you can expect to live. Now imagine how you would feel if you knew you were going to die in two years from now. What would you do differently with your life?

4. Now think about how precious your life is. Who would you want to tell that you loved them? What would you want to do with your remaining time? Would you want to get closer to your family and friends? Would you quit your job and travel?

5. After about 10 minutes of asking yourself questions, spend another 10 minutes writing down everything you imagined you would do and how it would make you feel. Make doing these things a priority in your life today.

WORKAHOLISM

What used to be called "workaholism" is fast becoming
the norm for white collar workers. Long hours and
taking work home is expected if you want to compete
in the corporate world. This meditation helps you to
find a better alternative.

1. Prepare by writing down your typical schedule for a week.

2. Sit on a cushion or chair in your meditation space. Meditate by watching your breath for 5 minutes.

3. Now look over your schedule. How much time did you spend with your loved ones or friends? Did you get 8 hours' sleep a night? When did you relax and play during the week? Did you eat well and exercise? Did you tend to your spiritual life? Are you using your hectic schedule to avoid intimacy? How much money are you really making an hour?

4. Now contemplate your long term goals. What kind of life do you really want? What do you want to achieve? When you are on your deathbed, how do you want to have spent your life?

5. Think about the qualities you would like to manifest in your life. Do you want warmth, love, fun, play, spiritual development and time in nature? How is your current life helping you have these experiences? What changes can you make to bring more of what you want into your life?

6. End your meditation by affirming what is most important to you and committing to creating a more balanced and rewarding life.

HIGH ROAD

If you are facing a difficult decision, where "doing the
right thing" may have negative consequences, it may
be hard to follow your moral and ethical principles.
This meditation will help you take the "high road"
if that is what you choose to do, and will help you
live according to your values.

1. Sit on a cushion or chair and meditate by watching your breath for 5 minutes.

2. Bring to mind the situation that is troubling you. If there were no negative consequences, what would you do? What action would feel most congruent with your values? Visualize yourself talking to whomever you need to and taking any action you feel appropriate.

3. Visualize the same situation, but this time bring to mind any negative consequences that may come your way if you do what you feel is right. Imagine how you will feel if you lost your job or your friend? Would you feel more comfortable if you acted in line with how you would like to live your life? Would acting on your principles help some and harm others?

4. Sometimes there are no black or white answers, but spending time quietly trying out ethical decisions is the best way to come to know what is best. Ask your higher power to help you make the most compassionate decision for yourself and anyone else involved.

MAKE PEACE WITH MONEY

Money – making it, having it, wanting it – is central
to most people's lives and a source of great anxiety for
many. This meditation helps you make peace with money
by putting it in perspective. It reduces anxiety about
money and promotes a less materialistic view of life.

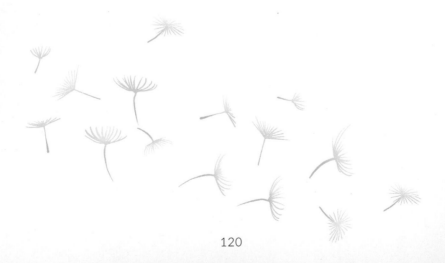

1. In preparation, write about what money means to you and what role it plays in your life.

2. Sit on a cushion or chair in your meditation space. Make sure your space is private and quiet. Take a few deep breathes to clear your mind and relax your body.

3. Review what you wrote down in preparation and put it aside. Explore how you feel when you have money. Do you feel more real or substantial? Do you feel you exist more solidly than when you don't have money?

4. Now imagine how you feel when you are broke. Do you feel diminished, deflated and less valuable as a person? Notice, in reality, you don't become more solid or less substantial when you have or don't have money. Contemplate how money functions as an idea causing you to feel more or less valuable.

5. Bring to mind ten things that are not measured in monetary terms. Your list might include the loving gaze of your partner, a wonderful conversation with a friend, the laughter of your child or the playfulness of your pet.

6. End your meditation by affirming that you are valuable with or without money. Commit to meditating on the meaning of money to help you counteract the cultural message of materialism. Seek out and value those precious experiences money can't buy.

DREAM MAP

Create a dream map for manifesting your dreams. Then meditate on your map to help your dreams come true. This meditation is great for when your everyday life is starting to feel a little stagnant, and for when you need to remind yourself of your true goals in life.

1. In preparation, find a stack of old magazines, brochures or other visual material. You will need a base for your map, a plain piece of paper the size you want your map to be. Then you will need scissors and glue. If you want to use other art supplies, gather those as well. Start finding images that symbolize what you would like to manifest in your life.

2. Find a quiet place where you can be alone. Spread out your materials on a table or on the floor. Sit quietly for a few minutes, breathe deeply and open your heart and mind to your deepest desires. Ask your higher power to help you to manifest dreams that are beneficial not only to you, but to the rest of the universe.

3. You may want to divide your dream map into areas, such as spiritual, physical, work, relationships or in any way that makes sense to you. Begin to arrange and paste down images that will serve as a reminder of your dreams. Draw, paint, add glitter or anything else that works for you.

4. When you have finished, ask your higher power to help you manifest the dreams you have visualized on your dream map. Place your dream map on a wall where you can see it every day. If you want to keep it private, put it in a drawer, but take it out every day, look at it and take action toward making your dreams come true.

FOUR DIRECTIONS

Many spiritual traditions invoke the four cardinal directions in their prayers and rituals. Practise this when you want to ground yourself in your environment.

1. Locate the cardinal directions using your compass. Stand with your spine straight. Take a deep breath. As you breathe, feel your heart expand and fill with warmth and exhale very slowly. Continue breathing in this way for a few minutes.

2. Now stand facing east. Offer thanks to the east for the water you drink, bathe in and cook with. Contemplate the importance of clean water in your life and for everyone else on the planet.

3. Rotate to face south. Offer thanks to the south for the Earth and the food you eat. Contemplate how lucky you are to have enough food. Offer your gratitude to the Earth for providing your daily nutrition.

4. Stand facing west. Offer thanks to the west for fire and the warmth it provides. Give thanks for hot water, heat in the winter, and the ability to cook your food. Contemplate how fire transforms your life on a daily basis.

5. Stand facing north and offer thanks to the north for the air you breathe. Take some deep breaths. Extend your belly then lift your diaphragm and allow the air to fill your lungs.

6. Now bring your focus to the centre where you are standing. Offer thanks for the environment in which you live. Take a moment to enjoy the state of gratitude you have evoked. Take a deep breath into your heart and exhale.

PATH OF GRACE

This meditation helps you bring the Divine's grace to your everyday life. Try this meditation when you want to turn your life around, and live it in accordance with the Divine's grace, as you understand it.

1. Sit on a cushion or chair in your meditation space. Light a candle. Breathe deeply for a few minutes to centre and calm your mind.

2. Think of past times in your life when you felt the Divine's grace intervening when least expected. Contemplate how you can be more receptive to grace and make room for grace to enter your life. How can you extend the grace you have been given to your family, friends and community? In this world where everything is pushed to its limits and people are emotionally, financially and physically stressed, it is important to help relieve the pressure and create the space for grace to enter. How can you reorganize your priorities so that you can accommodate the needs of your circle for tenderness and grace?

3. Decide on three ways in which you can follow the path of grace. For example, you might invite a friend with whom you have had a falling-out for dinner. Ask your partner how you can be a better partner. Get involved in helping the elderly in your community.

4. End your meditation by composing a prayer to the Divine, thanking them for all their blessings.